FEB 1 3 2004

W9-AVJ-970

FEMALE FIGURE SKATING LEGENDS

Oksana Baiul

Nicole Bobek

Ekaterina Gordeeva

Nancy Kerrigan

Michelle Kwan

Tara Lipinski

Katarina Witt

Kristi Yamaguchi

CHELSEA HOUSE PUBLISHERS

EKATERINA GORDEEVA

Pegi Deitz Shea

CHELSEA HOUSE PUBLISHERS
Philadelphia

Produced by Choptank Syndicate, Inc.

Editor and Picture Researcher: Norman L. Macht
Production Coordinator and Editorial Assistant: Mary E. Hull
Design and Production: Lisa Hochstein

CHELSEA HOUSE PUBLISHERS

Editor in Chief: Stephen Reginald
Managing Editor: James Gallagher
Production Manager: Pamela Loos
Art Director: Sara Davis
Photo Editor: Judy L. Hasday
Senior Production Editor: Lisa Chippendale
Publishing Coordinator: James McAvoy
Cover Illustration: Keith Trego

Cover Photos: AP/Wide World Photos

The Chelsea House World Wide Web site address is
http://www.chelseahouse.com

First Printing

1 3 5 7 9 8 6 4 2

Library of Congress Cataloging-in-Publication Data

Shea, Pegi Deitz.
    Ekaterina Gordeeva / Pegi Deitz Shea.
      p.   cm. — (Female figure skating legends)
    Includes bibliographical references (p.) and index.
    Summary: A biography of skating star Ekaterina Gordeeva who,
with her husband Sergei Grinkov, won two Olympic gold medals,
and who, since his untimely death in 1995, skates alone.
    ISBN 0-7910-5027-0 (hc.)
    1. Gordeeva, Ekaterina—Juvenile literature. 2. Skaters—Russia (Federation)—
Biography—Juvenile literature. 3. Grinkov, Sergei, 1967-1995—Juvenile literature.
[1. Gordeeva, Ekaterina. 2. Ice skaters. 3. Grinkov, Sergei, 1967–1995. 4. Women—
Biography.] I. Title. II. Series.
GV850.G67S54   1998
796.91'2'029—dc21
    [B]   98-25571
                                                                                   CIP
                                                                                    AC

CONTENTS

HARMONY IN LIFE

In the summer of 1993 Katia Gordeeva and Sergei Grinkov went into training in Ottawa, Canada, for the 1994 winter Olympics to be held in Lillehammer, Norway. They had been skating together for 12 years, since she was 11 and he was 16, beginning when they were students in a rigid, demanding school for skaters in their native Russia.

Over the years they had fallen in love and been transformed from two skaters into a pair so close they seemed physically as well as spiritually bonded on the ice. They had married in 1991 and had a year-old daughter, Daria. They had gained international stardom but not without illness, accidents, frustrations, and painful decisions along the way.

Gordeeva and Grinkov, shown during their long program at the 1994 Olympics, had an ease and grace that came from having skated together since childhood.

On the platform in Hamar, Norway, in 1994, Gordeeva and Grinkov smile after receiving their second gold medals for pairs figure skating. The pair won their first Olympic gold in 1988.

They had begun their training for the Olympics reluctantly, having left Daria in Russia with Katia's mother. But their spirits lifted when the grandmother brought the child to be with them in the fall. They loved coming home after an exhausting day of practice to relax with the baby they called Dasha. Sergei enjoyed taking Dasha onto the ice, holding her by the waist as she slid gleefully between his legs.

Their coach, Marina Zueva, choreographed a lively flamenco dance for the pair's short program, and for contrast selected Beethoven's "Moonlight Sonata" for the long program. They would skate in formal, navy blue velvet with white collars and a white stripe down the middle of the costumes.

Marina sought to present Sergei as "celebrating woman as the mother of all mankind." To Katia, the music expressed "what changes love can bring about in people, how it can make them stronger."

Waiting to go onto the ice for their first appearance in Norway, Katia looked at a picture of Dasha and thought about her parents in Moscow. But once she was out on the ice, all her concentration focused on Sergei. They would skate not for their country, not for the nameless blur of faces in the audience, not for the gold, but just for themselves.

A sound performance in the short program, completing all the required moves and jumps, put them in first place going into the long event. When their turn came, Katia and Sergei became one with the music and each other. Their arms and legs lined up perfectly. They entered and finished each athletic jump with balletic grace. In moves borrowed from the more intimate sport of ice dancing, Katia wrapped herself around her partner. She posed almost straight upside down in a one-handed lift, and landed both her double Axels, the jump that had always given her the most trouble.

While everything went perfectly for Katia, Sergei missed the second jump of a side-by-side combination early in the performance. He did only one revolution of his double Salchow instead of his scheduled two. It was the first mistake he had ever made in competition. For a fleeting second they wondered how much it would cost them.

Despite these errors, eight of the nine judges placed them first. American judge Elaine DeMore explained, "They were skating as one. But it's the inner connection between them that shines. . . . All their overhead moves are done at smooth, quiet speed. It's so peaceful."

An American coach, John Hicks, described them as "the consummate pair. You can't appreciate the capacity of a 180-pound man to move across the ice without a sound until you watch him skate. They are a symphony for the senses."

Standing together to receive their gold medals, Gordeeva and Grinkov seemed in perfect harmony not only with each other, but with the universe.

RUSSIAN LIFE

Ekaterina Gordeeva (ay-cat-er-EE-na gor-dee-AY-va) was born May 28, 1971, in Moscow, the capital and the largest city of the former Soviet Union, now Russia.

Katia (KAHT-ya) received her athletic abilities and discipline from her father. Alexander Alexeyevich Gordeev (a-LEX-ay-i-vich GOR-dee-ayf) performed with the famous Moiseyev Dance Company as one of the folk dancers who squat and, arms folded, kick their legs out one at a time. He also jumped over flashing swords.

Katia admired her mother, Elena Levovna (eh-LAY-na le-VOV-na), above all people. A tele-type operator for the Soviet news agency, Tass, Elena gave Katia her beauty, pride, balance, and athletic poise.

St. Basil's Cathedral rises out of Red Square in Moscow, where Ekaterina Gordeeva was born.

Since both parents traveled often, Elena's parents lived with the family and took care of Katia and her younger sister, Maria. The girls called their grandmother "Babushka" and their grandfather "Diaka."

Katia loved it when Babushka read to her from the scary *Grimm's Fairy Tales*. She helped her grandmother cook, sew, and knit. For her favorite holiday, Easter, Katia helped Babushka suck the yolks out of eggs and decorate the shells.

Her Diaka, a celebrated World War II colonel, shared his history and geography books with Katia. At their dacha (DAH-cha), a summer home north of Moscow, Katia loved fishing with Diaka. Her favorite activity was collecting wild mushrooms with him in the nearby pine and birch forests. Katia preferred her mushrooms pickled or fried in patties.

Katia spent her happy childhood days playing and staging war scenes with neighborhood friends. She enjoyed painting, playing with dolls, and doing crafts and needlepoint. She also choreographed dances and plays that she and Maria would perform for their family and friends. Katia liked being the director of these plays and sometimes bossed her little sister around. She later wondered if she had been imitating her demanding father.

When Katia was four, a skater with the Central Red Army Club (CSKA) had persuaded Alexander Gordeev to let Katia try out for the prestigious skating club. Despite being a year younger than the required age, and wearing skates five sizes too big, Katia made the club.

The army skating clubs, funded by the Communist government, produced many world and Olympic champions. The clubs excelled in nurturing pairs, teaming skaters at a much younger age than other countries did. They also

kept the pairs together longer; many of them later married. The skaters' parents did not have to pay for ice time, coaches, and travel, expenses that often ran from $25,000 to $50,000 a year in the United States.

At an age when most children learn to ride a bike with training wheels, Katia began skating twice a week. When she turned five, she began skating four times a week. Three times a week, she did a workout of stomach and leg exercises and jumping. She also practiced ballet three times a week so the beauty of her skating would add grace to her athletic skill.

Even though the government made skating affordable, Katia's family faced many demands. Tired from their own jobs, sometimes her parents wouldn't get up at 5:30 A.M. to take her to skating practice. Katia would wake them. "I can't miss it," she told them. "It's my job." This determination and will would motivate and guide Katia through her life on and off the ice.

Katia's father was a member of the Moiseyev Dance Company, shown above. Male members of the Moiseyev display the leaping skills for which Russian folk dancers are renowned.

Members of a Red Army club drill in Moscow's Red Square.

Wearing a brown uniform dress with a black apron and white lace collar, Katia began school when she was seven. All children who showed promise in sports attended a 10-grade sports school. While taking regular academic classes, they also trained in their specialty. However, if the children did not improve in their sports, they were not promoted in that school. When Katia began, 40 children in her class skated at CSKA. When she graduated at the age of 16, only 10 skaters remained—five boys and five girls.

The club staged a competition, a test, at the end of each school year in May. While Katia always passed, she began to realize that she couldn't jump as well as other girl skaters.

Katia's father wanted her to become a ballet dancer. When she was 10 years old, he arranged a ballet school tryout. Katia failed.

"She did everything not to enter that school," her father emphasized in a television interview. Katia even admitted that she didn't try her best.

Fortunately, a skating coach recognized Katia's talent and will. "Don't worry," he told her. He had grand plans for her skating.

The next year she and her friend Oksana Koval were invited to skate at a rink where the pairs and boy skaters practiced. Katia felt proud. She knew the coaches were considering the girls as potential pairs partners.

Among the boy skaters, Katia recognized Sergei Mikhailovich Grinkov (SIR-gay mi-KAYL-uh-vich GREEN-cof), a dark-haired, blue-eyed boy. She had noticed that he acted differently from the others in school. He got away with wearing stylish blazers and ties instead of a uniform. He carried a briefcase, not a shoulder bag. But Katia had never talked to Sergei, who was four years older than she.

Unlike her ballet tryout, Katia tried her best that day on the rink. Her friend Oksana became a ballerina. When she returned to school the following September, Katia discovered that she had been chosen to skate pairs. She wondered who her partner would be.

FIRST AND ONLY PARTNER

Vladimir Zaharov (VLAD-i-meer ZAH-ha-rof),
a former pairs skater who became a pairs
coach, saw a perfect match between Katia and
Sergei Grinkov.

When the two young skaters met, Katia was
nervous and excited. "It was an amazing experience," she told a television interviewer. "I was
very shy. I didn't look at him at all."

Sergei was born February 4, 1967, and
raised in an apartment near the Moscow River.
His parents, Anna Filipovna (fil-i-POHV-na)
and Mikhail Kondrateyevich (kon-dra-TAY-i-
vich), both worked long hours as policemen, so
Sergei spent days and nights at daycare centers.
His older sister Natalia often took care of him.
Growing up, Sergei enjoyed swimming, soccer,

---

*Katia had to learn how to skate with her body close
to Sergei Grinkov's.*

17

tennis, and hockey, and he especially liked playing with toy soldiers during his bathtime.

"When he was five, he was placed in the Army Club School and those crazy training sessions began," Natalia told a television interviewer.

Despite the rigorous schedule, Sergei Grinkov enjoyed himself. His friend Alexander Fadeev (FAH-dee-ef), also a skater, said Sergei was rarely serious, always having fun.

Katia and Sergei had much to learn. Skating pairs is very different from skating singles, even though many moves and jumps are the same. In pairs, judges examine how closely the two skaters are aligned, and how smoothly they glide while in each other's hands or arms. Judges want the skaters to move as one. The skaters' legs must extend at precisely the same angle. The timing of their jumps, spins, and footwork must match.

Katia was 45 pounds lighter than Sergei and didn't even reach his shoulder. Sergei had to shorten his strides and spin his larger body faster in order to keep up with his tiny partner.

Sergei and Katia also had to learn lifts, throws, and death spirals—moves not used in singles skating. In a lift, the man swoops the woman up into the air and holds her in a ballet-like position above his head. Often he uses only one arm to support her. In a star lift, she poses with both arms gracefully in the air.

Coach Zaharov, concerned about Sergei's strength, made his young skater practice lifting an awkward iron chair over his head. If Sergei made a mistake, better that he drop a chair than drop Katia. She, too, worked on strengthening her hands and wrists by winding a bar attached to a weight. While Katia always felt safe in Sergei's arms for lifts, she feared the throws. In this dangerous move, the woman jumps, is swiftly lifted by her partner, then thrown through the air. After spinning two or three times, she must land on one foot.

The throws can disorient the woman because she ends up jumping farther than if she were jumping alone. The woman can fly 10 feet, spinning all the while. She lands not only with her own force, but also with the speed created by her partner.

Katia often fell when they were first learning throws. Although one coach instructed Sergei to throw Katia as if she were a crystal vase, Katia herself felt like a rag doll. When she would fall, Sergei would cringe and beg her to take a break. Despite feeling nauseated with dread of the throws, Katia never stopped until she got it right.

Another difficult move the pair had to learn was the death spiral, in which the man pivots

Todd Sands and Jeni Meno perform a pairs throw. This move scared Katia when she was first learning to skate with Sergei, as she often fell.

One of the most difficult pairs moves Sergei and Ekaterina had to learn was the death spiral, which they demonstrate here. Katia's head is just inches from the ice as Sergei spins her.

and pulls the woman in a circle. Spiraling down to the ice, then back up, the woman skates on one foot. She arches her back so that her head skims dangerously close to the rock-hard ice.

When done correctly, the death spiral makes it look as if the man is pulling the woman up over the edge of a cliff. When Sergei or Katia leaned back too far, they would both crash to the ice. (One reason most female skaters wear flesh-colored leg tights is to hide the bruises they receive during practice.)

In addition to these special pairs techniques, Katia and Sergei had to practice side-by-side jumps including Axels, Salchows, toe loops, Lutzes, and flips, and moves including cross-overs, camels, and spread eagles.

After a year, Katia and Sergei had a new coach. They also began working with a choreographer named Marina Zueva (zoo-AY-va), who designed their dance moves and selected their music.

While the pair would have many coaches throughout the years, Marina Zueva became the most consistent professional and personal force in their skating life. Katia would sometimes feel jealous about the special bond Marina had with Sergei when they discussed books, art, and politics.

Schooled at the National Theater Institute in Moscow, Marina taught Katia and Sergei to create drama on the ice. Her long black hair swinging, her red nails flashing, Marina would describe movements to the young skaters and softly position their hands. She asked them to make faces in a mirror so they could see how their features expressed emotions. Marina also suggested similes to help Katia and Sergei understand the mood and personality of the music. She asked them to imagine themselves as flowers, soar like birds, or prance like animals.

After working only three months with their new coach and choreographer, the pairs team of Gordeeva and Grinkov made their international debut. They traveled to compete in Sapporo, Japan, in December 1983. The huge rink filled with spectators made Katia nervous. Skating in matching red outfits, the pair missed a few jumps but finished sixth—not bad for their first Junior World Championships.

In December 1984 they traveled to the United States for the first time, to skate in the Junior World Championships in Colorado Springs. Katia and Sergei fed ducks in ponds and bought Christmas ornaments. They celebrated their unexpected victory by buying gifts to bring home to Russia. Running out of money, they bartered Russian nesting dolls for more American souvenirs.

Just a year earlier, Katia had regarded Sergei as a big brother. Now at the age of 13, she found herself feeling uncomfortable when Sergei flirted with the older girl skaters. It made her happy to see him always carrying a keychain she'd given him. And when they horsed around in a massive snowball fight, Katia admitted to herself that she enjoyed being around Sergei off, as well as on, the ice.

4

TOUGH LITTLE CROCUS

Like a crocus that emerges just before a huge snowstorm, Katia's blooming fairy tale was quickly trampled. The blizzard's name was Stanislav Alexeyvich Zhuk (zook), head coach of CSKA.

Zhuk appointed himself the new coach of Gordeeva and Grinkov. Then he designed artless, mechanical programs for them to skate, discarding the lively programs that Marina had created to the music of American composers Scott Joplin, Duke Ellington, and Louis Armstrong.

Katia feared Zhuk, who spied on her and Sergei and made them record their movements in journals. He used his power to verbally and physically abuse both female and male skaters. Reeking of alcohol, Zhuk terrorized the skaters

Wearing red costumes trimmed in gold, Gordeeva and Grinkov dance to the opera Carmen *for their short program at the 1988 Olympics in Calgary. Every Olympic judge placed the couple first.*

with his deeply set eyes, rough hands, and filthy talk.

However she despised Zhuk, Katia still had to obey him. If she didn't, she risked getting kicked out of the club and school. Because Sergei had already finished school, he could get away with naps and fun during his personal time. But Katia couldn't. She found comfort in the huge white and brown stuffed dog Sergei had given her for her 14th birthday. She and Sergei found relief by making faces and imitating Zhuk behind his back. Katia said Zhuk had tried to separate Sergei and her off the ice. However, dealing with the overbearing coach just made Katia and Sergei grow closer.

Most teenagers enjoy hanging out with their friends and participating in activities after school. In 1986, Katia's daily schedule looked like this: two-and-a-half hours of practice in the

When Grinkov and Gordeeva, or "G&G," as they became known, first entered the pairs skating arena, their toughest competitors were the renowned Russian pair Elena Valova and Oleg Vasiliev, shown here.

morning, school, homework, then three hours of practice at night.

Zhuk also arranged special training sessions at a Black Sea beach, with no sunbathing or horseplay allowed. Zhuk filled their days with running, boulder-tossing sessions, stair-running, and snorkeling, all designed to build endurance and strength. Katia, a weak swimmer, soon grew to hate the seashore.

Katia's will to succeed and her dedication to training didn't allow time for friends with whom she could talk, especially about boys. Later she wrote, "It's a void in my life that I'll never be able to fill."

Zhuk's regimented strategy did pay off for the country. In their first senior-level competition, the 1986 Soviet Union Nationals, Gordeeva and Grinkov came in second to Elena Valova (va-LOH-va) and Oleg Vasiliev (va-SEE-lee-ev), the defending world champions. Shortly after, at the European Championships in Copenhagen, Gordeeva and Grinkov placed second again. Spectators wondered who they were; their names were not even on the program.

Figure skating fans all over the world would soon know the names "Gordeeva and Grinkov." At the 1986 World Championships—their first senior World competition—the two youngsters took advantage of mistakes made by other pairs. Dressed in pink-trimmed white outfits, Gordeeva and Grinkov surged into first place by skating what the *New York Times* called a "lively and well-synchronized" performance.

Pressure overcame Katia, who broke down in tears when their victory was announced. "The whole season was overwhelming," Katia said in a television interview. "The world was too stressful for us."

Displaying the style that made them famous, Gordeeva and Grinkov smile at the crowd during the 1987 Worlds in Cincinnati, Ohio, where the couple won their second World gold.

Sergei told some friends that he did not enjoy skating anymore. When asked why he still did it, Sergei replied, "Because I have to."

But like the tough little crocus bulb that survives winter to bloom every year, Katia stood up to Zhuk and her father, who had supported Zhuk. Marina Zueva, Katia, Sergei, and other skaters petitioned CSKA to remove Zhuk as head coach. CSKA allowed Zhuk to keep his title but appointed the gentle Stanislav Vitorovich Leonovich (STAN-eh-slav vik-TOR-o-vich lee-ON-o-vich) as the new coach for Katia and Sergei. Marina Zueva was also welcomed back, and she returned the joy of skating to the young pair.

Skating fans would soon embrace Gordeeva and Grinkov following a strange event at the 1987 European Championships in Sarajevo. Videotaped scenes of this program would air

around the world and become part of the pair's legend.

As the couple skated, a short strap at the bottom of Sergei's pants broke and began flapping. The skating referee blew his whistle for the pair to stop. Confused, they kept skating. The referee then stopped the music. But Coach Leonovich motioned for them to continue skating in the completely silent arena. The fans, amazed at the pair's determination, stood and began to clap in unison. Katia and Sergei finished, flawlessly, to a thunderous ovation.

However, the judges refused to score the performance. They demanded that Katia and Sergei skate the whole program again. The audience answered with jeering whistles and boos. Exhausted and disappointed, Gordeeva and Grinkov refused to repeat the program. The judges disqualified them.

Katia admitted that their team made a mistake in not halting the performance when the whistle blew and the music stopped. The mistake made the pair more determined than ever. "It made us angry as we prepared for the 1987 World Championships in Cincinnati," she wrote. Ablaze in scarlet costumes trimmed with gold, Katia and Sergei skated their best ever and defended their world pairs title.

"I was very very proud of all of us—not of me—but all of us," Katia said in a television interview.

The rewards for winning championships and Olympic medals are skating tours. Winners pile onto buses, travel from city to city, and are paid to perform more enjoyable and less strenuous exhibitions. Until the early 1990s, athletes hoping to compete in the Olympics were not supposed to accept prize money for their wins. But the rules were starting to change.

Katia and Sergei were invited by Tom Collins, a former American skater, to join his Campbell Soup Tour of World Figure Skating Champions. The tour performed in 25 American cities in one month.

Despite the hectic schedule, Katia threw herself into the tourist scene. She saw *Phantom of the Opera* on Broadway. She ate at McDonald's. She and Sergei visited Disneyland. They also went to the movies, where Sergei began holding Katia's hand—not quite the same way he held it on the ice.

Sergei and Katia stand on the medal platform at the 1988 Olympics in Calgary. At right are their teammates and competitors, Elena Valova and Oleg Vasiliev.

That summer Katia and Sergei began training for the 1988 Winter Olympics in the western Canadian city of Calgary. Like all Olympic competitors, the pair was whisked off to train at elite athletic facilities. They took physical exams, practiced skating moves on and off the ice, ran miles and miles, and lifted tons of weights. But they were also pampered with the finest food, including caviar, which is rich in protein.

Katia fondly recalled this "dear" period with Sergei. "We had those quiet evenings when we could talk—not about skating."

However, in November the country's hopes of Olympic gold in the pairs competition crashed. Sergei's skate blade caught in the ice while he was holding Katia high in a lift. His grip faltered. Katia fell more than six feet and landed on her forehead. She spent six days in the hospital with a concussion.

Sergei brought roses to Katia and apologized, even though it was an accident. Seeing him so upset made Katia feel sorry for him. And when they returned to the ice, she noticed that he held her more firmly than ever, as if he would never let her go. Katia wrote, "Before we had been like two skaters. After that, we were a pair."

The pair's glue strengthened when Sergei was invited to Katia's home for Christmas, which many Russians celebrate on December 31. It was the first time Sergei had spent time with her family, and he acted shy. Katia made Sergei a needlepoint clown as a gift. And she made a wish: to skate well at the Olympics.

The pair's experience in Calgary got off to a rocky start. Sergei came down with a stomach flu and could not eat anything for two days. Katia, on the other hand, was so worried, nervous, and homesick, she kept gobbling down cheesecake in the Olympic Village cafeteria.

When Sergei recovered, Gordeeva and Grinkov performed an almost-perfect short program to "The March of the Toreadors," from the opera *Carmen*. For their long program, they changed to a lyrical medley of Chopin and Mendelssohn. To match the music, the couple wore sky blue costumes with sequins and white flowers vining up the left sides of their bodies.

During the performance, Katia and Sergei's faces took on looks of wonder. Their eyes remained wide, their lips parted in joyful smiles. Instead of winding down at the end of their four-minute program—as many skaters do—they finished strongly. They performed side-by-side jump combinations, and Sergei held Katia aloft with one hand while he twirled breezily halfway down the ice.

Dick Button, former Olympic champion from the U.S., noted that Sergei was almost a foot taller and weighed almost twice as much as Katia, who was five feet tall and weighed 84 pounds. Button said that Sergei could send Katia through the air "as if she were shot out of a cannon."

In an editorial entitled "Peerless Pair," the *New York Times* proclaimed: "When Grinkov threw Gordeeva into the air, she returned to the ice as lightly as the bird lands on the branch."

Ekaterina Gordeeva, 16, and Sergei Grinkov, 21, won the gold medal with every single judge placing them first. Katia's Christmas wish had come true. Katia felt proud and wanted to celebrate and prolong the moment of triumph. But that evening all the older coaches and skaters—Sergei included—had gone out on the town without her.

Before the Olympics, Katia had promised herself a huge ice cream sundae if they won the gold. Again she was disappointed. The game room, with the gleaming ice cream fountain, unending flavors, and mounds of toppings, had already closed.

Alone and angry, draped in her gold medal, the Olympic champion sat in the cafeteria and ate three bowls of regular ice cream. Would Katia always be regarded as a child?

TRIPLE TOE LOVE

Back in Russia after their Olympic triumph, Katia's parents took Sergei and Katia north to a friend's house on the Volga River, where they had fun snowmobiling, talking, and dining together.

After the excitement of the Olympics the pair soon had to return to the reality of training. At the World Championships in Budapest, Hungary, Katia skated with a third partner— the flu. Sick and exhausted, she fell trying to land a triple Salchow throw.

Then they were off on another skating tour to 25 European cities. Katia and Sergei always sat together and talked on the bus rides. She also spent time with the married couples. But whenever the older skaters went out

Publicly declaring their love for each other for the first time, Ekaterina and Sergei show their feelings on ice at the 1989 World Championships in Paris.

and explored the cities, Katia found herself left behind.

Hurt and a bit jealous of Sergei's friendships, Katia finally told him, "You could have at least asked me. . . . Maybe I'd like to go, too."

Tom Collins asked Katia and Sergei to join his Campbell Soup Tour again, but Katia felt too tired and homesick. She relaxed, instead, with her parents on a two-week vacation at a Black Sea resort. Back in Moscow, Katia attended a banquet given for Ronald Reagan, then president of the United States. She sat with him and with Raissa Gorbachev, wife of the Soviet president Mikhail Gorbachev. Without Sergei, though, Katia felt bored. Nobody talked to the 16-year-old girl.

For Katia's 17th birthday, Sergei gave her perfume and flowers. Katia didn't need these sophisticated gifts to remind her that she was becoming a woman. Suddenly, it seemed, she had grown to 5'1" and 95 pounds.

Highly trained female athletes, including gymnasts and long-distance runners, often experience puberty late because they have low levels of body fat. This is true especially for girls who are as petite as Katia. Just as hormones can cause mood swings in 11- to 14-year-olds, they can affect a 17-year-old too. She missed not having friends her own age and began behaving rudely to her coaches.

But she soared when Sergei told her he liked her just the way she was. And when she lost her temper, he gently encouraged her to be strong and not to show weakness to anyone. "I saw in Sergei . . . what I was looking for in myself: confidence, stability, maturity," Katia wrote in her memoir.

In November 1988 Katia suffered a stress fracture in her right foot. She wore a cast for

Dressed in the costumes of Romeo and Juliet, Ekaterina and Sergei wave to the crowd after winning the gold medal at the 1990 World Figure Skating Championships in Halifax, Nova Scotia. It was the couple's fourth World gold medal.

a month and spent another month off the ice. To help pass the time and take her mind off her misery, she studied English with a tutor twice a week. She looked forward to Sergei's daily visits or phone calls.

One day in December after her cast came off, Katia watched Sergei skate a new program. She began to panic, wondering if Sergei had found a new partner. Sergei calmed her by skating to her, swooping her up, and skating with her in his arms all through the program Marina had

G&G's choreographer, Marina Zueva, incorporated the couple's love into a "Romeo and Juliet" skating theme that became one of their hallmarks. The couple wore costumes inspired by Shakespeare's lovers and danced to the music of Tchaikovsky's "Romeo and Juliet."

created for them. Katia said, "It was like flying, and my heart was beating so loudly I was sure he could hear it."

Sergei must have heard it. On New Year's Eve, Sergei surprised Katia with a visit and a kiss. Not a brotherly one on the forehead or on the cheek. A real kiss. And then another.

In wonder and disbelief, Katia later asked Sergei why he had chosen her—a skinny little girl. "Everything's going to be okay. I love you just the way you are, Katoosha."

Although "Katuuh" was Sergei's nickname for Katia, he used "Katoosha" for special times when they were alone. Katia usually called him "Serioque," and saved "Seriozha" for intimate moments.

Because of Katia's tender foot, Gordeeva and Grinkov did not compete in the 1989 European Championships. They skated a less difficult program—removing a double Axel jump—at the World Championships in Paris and still won.

Katia's favorite memories of that time were not of competition, however. She and Sergei walked the early springtime streets of Paris for hours. They toured the ancient Notre Dame Cathedral. They dined on the world's finest food. After months of keeping their relationship a secret, they allowed people to see them together. For the first time, Katia told Sergei she loved him.

Seeing love deepen the bond between the two, Marina Zueva created a new program. They would skate to Tchaikovsky's "Romeo and Juliet," inspired by Shakepeare's play about two young lovers from rival families.

For the 1990 European and World Championships, Katia and Sergei looked as if they had stepped out of 16th century Verona, Italy. Katia took to the ice in a flowing white dress with a pale pink skirt. Sergei wore a maroon tunic with white ballooning sleeves over black pants.

Katia and Sergei looked, felt, and skated the part of Shakespeare's "star-cross'd" lovers. But their performances on the ice were star-crossed too. At the Europeans, Katia missed a double Axel and slipped in the death spiral. At the Worlds, she landed on two feet in her triple toe loop and fell on the double Axel.

The veteran Olympic champion Scott Hamilton said in the television broadcast of the Worlds,

"This must be the weakest performance I've ever seen them do in two years—maybe ever."

Despite the performances, Gordeeva and Grinkov won the gold medal in both competitions. Often, defending champions and top skaters are "held up" (given high enough marks to win) by the judges. The judges respect the champions' history of success more than they reward the freshness of young skaters or the flash of inconsistent skaters.

By 1990 the year-in, year-out competition, training, and touring began putting emotional and physical strain on Katia and Sergei. In Washington, D.C., their friend Viktor Petrenko broke the news that Sergei's father had just suffered a fatal heart attack in Moscow. Sergei flew home.

Then came a coaching change. Tatiana Tarasova (tah-tee-YAH-na ta-rah-SO-va) replaced Leonovich. Marina Zueva left, feeling she couldn't work with Tarasova, also a choreographer. In addition, pain in Sergei's shoulder worsened to the point that he needed surgery.

With an offer coming from the American talent agency, International Management Group, Sergei suggested to Katia, "Let's turn pro before we get so sick of the ice we can't look at it."

The bright spot of the year for Katia was being baptized in her family's Russian Orthodox faith. Father Nikolai, a gentle, gray-bearded priest, performed the private ceremony in a chapel next to the Church of Vladimir the Conqueror in Moscow.

While performing in Garmisch, Germany, Katia and Sergei bought an emerald and diamond antique engagement ring. Katia vowed she would never remove it from her hand.

They were married in a civil ceremony on April 20, 1991, and a church wedding at Father

Nikolai's chapel on April 28 came as a relief to their new and chaotic life. Skating friends from all over the world flew to Moscow to help them celebrate. "Gorka! Gorka!" they kept shouting to make the bride and groom kiss.

When it came time for Sergei and Katia to dance as husband and wife, they became embarrassed. After eight years of skating together, they didn't know how to dance with each other.

LIFE CHANGES

For eight years, since she was 11, Katia had led a totally regimented life. Her schedule, performances, and diet had been dictated down to the smallest detail. Now, in deciding to turn professional, Katia had to grow up fast. By asking for more control over her life, she unknowingly asked for more responsibility and stress. And she got it. "Suddenly, I was in charge of airplane tickets, the passports, the cash," Katia wrote.

In each city where they performed, Katia had to figure out how to shop, bank, travel, and communicate in different languages. She knew only beginner's English; Sergei spoke only Russian. She constantly feared that they would miss a flight, take the wrong bus, or lose everything they had.

After the birth of their daughter, Daria, Ekaterina had to work hard to regain her mastery of the ice. Here she skates with Sergei at the 1994 European Championships in Copenhagen.

Champion men's figure skater Scott Hamilton became a close friend of Gordeeva and Grinkov.

At first the strain overwhelmed her. Then her confidence returned, and a new thirst for fun grew. She began to fill up her newly won free time during their ice tours. In South Africa, Katia and Sergei shopped for furniture for their apartment, went on a safari, and visited a slum called a shantytown. In Aspen, Colorado, they enjoyed the bookstores where customers could relax with books in front of a fire. In Barcelona, they played soccer and ate fine Spanish food.

Most of all, Katia cherished the friendships she now had time to develop with other skaters. She and Sergei grew especially close to Scott Hamilton, the champion who had overcome a childhood disease.

Gordeeva and Grinkov, nicknamed "G&G" by their new friends, grew professionally, too. Directed by Tarasova, they wove even more acting into their performances, such as "West Side Story" and "Opera Piazza." A rendition of Tchaikovsky's *The Nutcracker*, choreographed by Canadian champion Toller Cranston, won G&G the World Professional Championships in 1991.

In January 1992 Katia began to fear that she was pregnant. "I was so young—twenty—and I was worried about missing a whole year of skating." But the encouragement of Sergei, Marina Zueva, and other friends soothed her. Father Nikolai told her that the child was "a gift from God . . . a child born from love."

Katia continued skating into her fifth month of pregnancy. Then she took the summer off to pamper herself and let others pamper her. To have the baby, they decided to return to the Princeton, New Jersey, hospital where Sergei's shoulder had been successfully repaired.

At 4:00 A.M., on September 11, 1992—nine days before her due date—Katia went into labor.

She called the hospital, and the receptionist told her to come right away. Sergei dropped Katia off at the emergency exit. Then he spent the next six hours waiting in the car. When the baby was about to come, a nurse fetched Sergei. He expected to see a brand new baby girl but was greeted with beeping machines spitting readouts.

Sergei kept kissing Katia's hand as she pushed. Soon Daria—five pounds, four ounces, red-faced, bald—entered the world. Sergei held

G & G wave to the crowd after receiving the gold medal for the pairs event at the European Figure Skating Championships held in Copenhagen in 1994.

her first. Then he telephoned to Russia to tell the new grandparents. Elena Levovna was surprised. She had planned on arriving in America before the birth to tell her daughter everything about babies.

Katia and Sergei were mesmerized by each little move "Dasha" made. With help from nurses and Katia's mother, the new parents learned how to diaper Dasha, bathe her, nurse her, and burp her. Sergei held Dasha's head still for her first passport photo. Daria Grinkova, one month old, became a dual citizen of Russia and the United States.

Twelve days after the birth, Katia accompanied Sergei to the gym. She had to work hard to shed the 18 pounds she had gained and regain the strength in her muscles. She tried skating on September 30. Still off balance, she fell on every jump. Nevertheless, skating felt like laughing with a good friend she hadn't seen in six months.

Katia and Sergei soon made one of the hardest decisions in their lives. In order to make a living, they had to leave their precious Daria behind with Elena for now. There was no way Dasha could thrive on her parents' gypsy schedule. Katia feared that Dasha would grow up knowing and loving her grandmother more than her own mother.

Back on tour, Katia and Sergei renewed their working relationship with Marina Zueva. Marina fixed up the Nutcracker program and G&G renewed their winning ways. Less than three months after the birth, the pair won their second World Professional Championship in 1992.

Marina suggested that they apply to become eligible for the 1994 Olympics. Many pro athletes—basketball players, track stars, skiers— were now being allowed to compete for their countries. The International Olympic Committee realized that it was impossible for an athlete to pay for the best training and compete without any money. The committee also admitted that it could not keep track of all monies made by all the athletes, and agreed to open the Olympics to pro skaters. This gave G & G the opportunity to seek a second gold medal. When they won in Norway in 1994, this time Katia went out with the group to celebrate.

DEATH SPIRAL

After the 1994 Olympics, Katia and Sergei set off on a tour of 65 American cities. While in America, they learned of a new training facility in Simsbury, a small town northwest of Hartford, Connecticut. If Katia and Sergei agreed to perform two free shows there a year, they would receive free ice time and a free condominium to live in. They could train with other skaters from the former Soviet Union who had moved there, and they would have a chance to build a more stable family life for themselves and their daughter Dasha.

Sergei and Katia moved to the 300-year-old town, only three hours from New York—their favorite city. They bought a Volvo station wagon and did their own grocery shopping. They enjoyed quiet, home-cooked dinners of

Tragedy struck in 1995 when Sergei Grinkov suffered a heart attack and collapsed on the ice during a practice session. Surrounded by family and friends, Katia and Sergei's mother attend his funeral.

spaghetti or dumplings, and they dined out at "Babushka," a restaurant created especially for the new Russian residents of Simsbury.

"Finally you're realizing that, yes, this is your man, your husband. He's also the father of your daughter," Katia told an interviewer as she reminisced about their life in Simsbury. "Those [times] will be the most important in my life."

Marina Zueva soon designed a program that would become Katia's favorite. Set to the music of Rachmaninoff, Katia and Sergei re-created poses found in Rodin's sculptures. All the poses showed lovers wrapped around each other. On the ice Katia and Sergei, dressed in earth colors, skated as if they wanted every part of themselves to touch. This program won them their third World Professional Championship in late 1994.

"What I found magical about this program was that every time we skated it, it was different," Katia commented. "Every night I heard the music as if for the first time."

The 1995 season kicked off with an exhausting 47-city Stars on Ice tour. Gordeeva and Grinkov skated love-song programs including the Rodin piece, Gershwin's "Crazy for You" and "Porgy and Bess," Ella Fitzgerald's "The Man I Love," and "Out of Tears" by The Rolling Stones.

The couple finally got to relax in their New England home just in time for spring. They sat back and watched Daria bloom along with the flowers.

The spring also gave Sergei time to rest his injured back, which was shooting pains all the way to his toes. Throughout the spring and summer, he and Katia heard a lot of advice and tried many different treatments. A doctor in Moscow said Sergei's back problem stemmed from too much air conditioning. So they stopped using it. A chiropractor in Odessa, Ukraine, adjusted Sergei's spine. It helped for a while, but Sergei's left foot grew numb. An American doctor drew fluid from Sergei's spine for a test and recommended physical therapy. Sergei exercised and swam nonstop, but still he had trouble putting any weight on his foot.

Then a trainer in Simsbury used a machine to stretch Sergei upside down. This relieved much of the pain and allowed Sergei to train again. The Stars on Ice skaters were working out in Lake Placid, New York. So the couple headed north and brought their stretching machine with them.

In the fall in Albany, New York, Gordeeva and Grinkov performed in the Skates of Gold III television show. They chose to do an easy program, Verdi's "Requiem," that wouldn't strain Sergei's back too much. "Requiem" means a celebration of a dead person's soul.

On November 20, Katia and Sergei were practicing the new program Marina had choreographed to Grieg's *Concerto in A Minor*. They did their side-by-side double flip cleanly. Sergei lifted Katia and threw her for a double Axel. Then Sergei stopped skating. Seeing him bent over, Katia skated to him. Sergei skated clumsily to the boards at the edge of the rink. He tried to hold on. But he couldn't. He slumped to the ice. And he didn't get up.

Katia kept asking him, "What's wrong?" But Sergei was unable to answer. Marina turned off the music, called 911, then began CPR on Sergei. While Marina worked to resuscitate him, Katia, now screaming, was comforted by fellow skaters Scott Hamilton, Kristi Yamaguchi, and Paul Wylie. An emergency medical team soon arrived and tried to restart the

28-year-old skater's heart. Then they put Sergei in the back of the ambulance. Katia sat in the front.

At the Adirondack Medical Center, doctors told Katia that Sergei had died. Katia went to him. She took off his skates and tried to warm his feet. She rubbed his hands, but they remained cold. She said she was sorry, but this time Sergei didn't tell her that everything was going to be all right.

Longtime friend Scott Hamilton reacted in shock to the news of Sergei's sudden death. "This is the healthiest person I know. He took care of himself."

"It's kind of hard to believe he's not going to come here again and say 'hi' to me," said Oksana Baiul, who lived next door to Gordeeva and Grinkov in Simsbury, Connecticut.

"I won't see him again," said Olympic skater Viktor Petrenko. "I don't see his smile."

Bob Young, president of the International Skating Center in Simsbury, said of Sergei and Katia, "Everything about them was as perfect as it gets. It just makes no sense at all."

An autopsy showed that two of Sergei's arteries had clogged. As a result, both the front half and the left side of his heart received no blood. Later reports would state that Sergei had the diseased heart of a 70-year-old man. He had inherited from his father a gene that caused his arteries to clog. Researchers have found this gene in other seemingly healthy men who have died young. A buildup of fatty deposits on Sergei's coronary arteries prevented his blood from flowing freely, and his heart had not received enough oxygen as a result.

Sergei, who always prefered Russia's ways, was taken back to Russia to be buried. However, Katia agreed to have funeral services

in New York state and Hartford, Connecticut, so Sergei's American friends could say goodbye. She tucked a picture of Daria into Sergei's coffin.

Back in Connecticut, Katia—numb and confused—was advised by a school psychologist to tell Daria the truth. Katia told her daughter, "Your father is dead; he's not coming back." Dasha didn't cry. She simply asked, "How can we see him?" Katia told Daria that she could always see him in her dreams. He was like an angel now.

Katia, surrounded by family and friends and Father Nikolai, buried Sergei in Vagankovsky Cemetery in Moscow on December 2, 1995. In the days that followed, Katia felt herself sinking to the ground as well. She felt she had no purpose. Her best friend, skating partner, and

Sergei Grinkov's death brought the skating community together in grief. Olympic skaters Scott Hamilton and Paul Wylie pay their respects as they pass by Grinkov's coffin at his funeral in Russia.

International Skating Center director Bob Young, Oksana Baiul, and her coach, Galina Zmievskaya, express their sorrow over the death of Sergei Grinkov.

husband was gone. Her family, thinking they were helping Katia, took control of Daria. Katia tried to distract herself by going out—to the symphony, galleries, the ballet—but she felt empty.

In mid-December, she asked Viktor Petrenko, a Ukranian skater who also trained in Simsbury, to send her skates from America. Back on the ice in an Army rink, Katia felt she could touch Sergei again. At first Katia said, she felt "a little heartachy," and she fell badly several times. But she felt that if her confidence and strength could return, it would only happen on the ice. "I can't draw, I can't write, I can't paint. I'm so happy to have a place to express my feelings," she told reporters.

That New Year's Eve, Katia laughed for the first time since Sergei's death. The healing had begun.

Marina Zueva and the skating community planned a tribute to Sergei in Connecticut. Encouraged by Father Nikolai, Katia decided to return to America, with Daria, and to try skating on her own.

I Skated
Not Alone

For "A Celebration of a Life" on February 27, 1996, the world's best skaters turned out to honor Sergei. They included Scott Hamilton, Katarina Witt, Kristi Yamaguchi, Oksana Baiul, Viktor Petrenko, Marina Klimova and Sergei Ponomarenko, Alexander Fadeev, and Brian Boitano.

Together the stars skated an opening procession (without Katia) to "Moonlight Sonata," the music to which G&G had won their second Olympic gold medal. Then the skaters performed individual programs. Oksana Baiul skated to "Ave Maria." Klimova and Ponomarenko skated to the same "Romeo and Juliet" music that Katia and Sergei had used. And at the end, the group recreated the Rodin sculptures that Sergei and Katia had brought to life.

Ekaterina Gordeeva takes the ice for the first time since her husband's death, at a 1996 tribute ceremony that honored the skating pair.

Standing alone behind a curtain at the edge of the Hartford rink while 16,000 spectators awaited her, Ekaterina Gordeeva realized she didn't have Sergei's eyes to look into anymore. He had been dead for three months. She felt unable to combine his power with her own.

Since she was 11, Katia had skated with her partner. She drew inspiration and strength from him. Her gray-blue eyes had never really sought the audience during a performance. They had only connected with her partner's. Now he was gone.

"We always kissed each other before we skated," she wrote in her memoir. "It was a terrible feeling to be standing there by myself."

Marina's choreography called for Katia to skate as if she were with Sergei for the last time, then as if he had been taken away from her. But Katia worried that her emotions would weaken her legs, and she would fall.

The first notes sounded Katia's cue to skate into the now darkened arena. Dressed in a filmy white costume that faded to blue-gray, Katia had felt so small. But now she felt "huge, suddenly, like I filled the entire ice. . . . I listened to Sergei. It was like I had double power."

Sergei had told her a long time ago not to show her weakness to anyone. Katia tamed her emotions and skated for five minutes—miming her loss, then rejoicing in the life she had shared with Sergei, a life she could continue. She punctuated this new hope by landing two jumps cleanly.

Katia skated for those "who have to start all over again, stand up from their knees." The crowd understood. It remained on its feet for the entire performance. At the end, the people cried through thunderous applause.

Katia's tears came too, though not from weakness. Smiling through her tears, she hugged Dasha, who had Sergei's bright blue eyes, and thanked the audience, her family, and her fellow skaters. And she thanked Sergei, who she felt had skated with her that night.

CBS broadcast commentator Verne Lundquist said, "In 30 years, it's the most moving event I've ever witnessed."

E. M. Swift, a writer for *Sports Illustrated*, wrote, "It was the greatest skating performance I'd ever seen."

New York Times reporter Richard Sandomir, who had bemoaned the glut of televised skating, called Katia's performance "stunning." And to see Katia clutch Daria at the end of the program "may turn hard hearts to mush."

Katia declared that her competing days were over, though she might continue skating in

Ekaterina hugs her daughter Daria after completing her solo performance at a tribute held in memory of her late husband Sergei Grinkov.

exhibitions as a solo. However, some of the tours staged competitions among the professionals. She wondered if she could measure up against singles champions. "It's fairly rare to succeed at both pairs and solo skating," said her friend and fellow skater Rosalyn Sumners.

With training, new choreography, and the same will that had guided Katia all her life, she transformed herself into a singles skater. In competition again, she regularly beat some of the best, often scoring higher than two-time Olympic singles champion Katarina Witt. In her first two scored events, she finished second to Kristi Yamaguchi. "People were mesmerized by [Katia]," said Brian Boitano. "They're thinking about her, not that they miss Sergei."

Olympic veteran Dick Button likened Katia to an "elegant snowflake, but one that is made of steel."

In addition to her touring, Katia worked closely with her manager and friend, Debbie Nast of International Management Group, to seek new business opportunities. She starred in several television specials, including "Snowden on Ice" and Disney's "Beauty and The Beast." She added commentary for the CBS broadcast of the 1998 Olympic figure skating. She helped create her own fragrance line, became a spokesperson for a retail chain, and co-authored a children's book, *A Letter for Daria*.

Katia enjoyed cooking and doing needlepoint in the five-bedroom home she shared with her parents. She shuttled Daria to school, skating practice, and friends' houses. She took time to enjoy her favorite foods—ice cream and sushi.

Talking about Sergei in her best-selling memoir, *My Sergei*, and the television special based on the book, helped ease Katia's pain. But she admitted that some days, "I wonder what I'm living for." Katia continued to see Sergei in her dreams, and she encouraged Dasha to see her father in the life around her.

Scott Hamilton said of the impact Gordeeva and Grinkov had on the world beyond skating, "Every performance they showed themselves. . . . Their time and their space is separate from the rest of skating history."

Ekaterina Gordeeva, like the tough and tiny crocus, continued to find ways to bloom.

CHRONOLOGY

1967   Sergei Grinkov born on February 4.

1971   Ekaterina Gordeeva born May 28 in Moscow.

1975   Learns to skate and is accepted into Central Red Army Skating Club.

1982   Paired with Sergei Grinkov.

1983   Begins working with choreographer Marina Zueva; she and Sergei win sixth place at the Junior World Championships.

1984   They win first Junior World Championship.

1986   They win second place at the European Championships; win first of two consecutive World Championships.

1987   They win second consecutive World Championship.

1988   Win gold medal at the Olympic Games.

1990   Gordeeva and Grinkov win second consecutive World Championship, for the second time; they turn professional.

1991   Sergei and Katia marry; win World Challenge of Champions and World Professional Championships.

1992   They repeat as World Professional Champions; daughter, Daria, born on September 11.

1994   Gordeeva and Grinkov win gold medal at the Olympic Games; they win World Professional Championship.

1995   Sergei Grinkov dies suddenly on November 20.

1996   Katia skates alone for the first time in an on-ice tribute to her late husband.

FURTHER READING

Brennan, Christine. *Inside Edge*. New York: Scribner, 1996.

Gordeeva, Ekaterina with E. M. Swift. *My Sergei: A Love Story*. New York: Warner Books, 1996.

MacLean, Norman. *Ice Skating Basics*. Englewood Cliffs, NJ: Prentice-Hall, Inc., 1984.

Petkevich, John Misha. *The Skater's Handbook*. New York: Charles Scribner's Sons, 1984.

Smith, Pohla. *Superstars of Women's Figure Skating*. Philadelphia, PA: Chelsea House Publishers, 1997.

ABOUT THE AUTHOR

Pegi Deitz Shea is the author of several award-winning children's books including *The Whispering Cloth* and *New Moon*. She teaches writing at the Institute of Children's Literature, and lives with her husband Tom, daughter Deirdre, and son Tommy in Connecticut.

ACKNOWLEDGEMENTS

The author thanks the members of the Wednesday Writers Group.

GLOSSARY

AXEL: a jump named for its inventor, Axel Paulsen. The Axel is the only jump launched while skating forward. A skater takes off from the forward outside skate edge and lands on the opposite foot on a back outside edge. A double Axel is the same jump with two and a half mid-air rotations. A triple Axel, achieved for the first time in 1978, requires three and a half mid-air rotations.

CAMEL: a skating spin performed with one leg extended back; the camel is called a flying camel when a skater jumps into the spin.

CROSSOVER: performed when a skater crosses his or her stride; a crossover tends to increase a skater's speed.

DEATH SPIRAL: a pairs figure skating move in which the man pivots and spins the woman in a circle around him with one hand while her arched body spirals down until it is almost parallel to the ice.

FLIP: a jump made by sticking the blade pick into the ice, revolving, and then landing on the back outside edge of the toe-assisting foot; the triple flip is the same jump with three revolutions.

FOOTWORK: any series of turns, steps, hops, and crossovers done at high speed.

LIFTS: pairs moves in which the man holds the woman up in a ballet-like position over his head; variations on lifts include the star lift, in which the woman holds both her arms in the air, and the one-armed lift, in which the man supports the woman with only one arm.

LOOP: a jump in which the skater takes off and lands on the same back outside edge.

LUTZ: a jump named for its creator, Alois Lutz. For the Lutz, a skater takes off on a back outside edge, revolves, and then lands on a back outside edge. When a skater revolves three times in the air, the jump is called a triple Lutz.

SALCHOW: a jump named after Swedish skater Ulrich Salchow. For the Salchow, a skater makes a long glide backward and then takes off on the outside edge of one skate, with a boost from the toe of the opposite skate. After revolving, the skater lands on the outside edge of the boosting skate. A double Salchow has two rotations; a triple Salchow requires three full rotations while in the air.

SPIN: a skater performs a spin by rotating from one fixed point; when skaters spin, they move so fast their image becomes blurred.

SIT SPIN: a spin in which the skater crouches down, balanced on one leg while the other extends; often a skater will pull up out of a sit spin to a standing spin position.

SPREAD-EAGLE: a move in which a skater glides on two feet, with the lead foot on a forward edge and the trail foot on the same edge, only backward.

TOE LOOP: a jump launched off the toe pick of the free foot in which a skater completes one rotation and lands on the back outside edge of the same foot. The toe pick can launch the skater to a great height; hence, a double toe loop has two mid-air rotations, and a triple toe loop has three.

THROWS: pairs moves in which the man throws the woman into the air, where she spins two or three times before landing on one foot.

INDEX

Picture Credits: AP/Wide World Photos: pp. 2, 6, 8, 10, 16, 19, 20, 26, 28, 32, 35, 40, 42, 43, 46, 51, 52, 54, 57, 60; New York Public Library: pp. 13, 14, 22, 24, 36